This book was produced with the generous assistance of

 Eastman Kodak Company

Library of Congress Cataloging-in-Publication Data

Baseball in America: from sandlots to stadiums, a portrait of
our national passion by 50 of today's leading photographers.
    p. cm.
    ISBN 0-00-215731-4
    1. Baseball—United States—Pictorial works.
    I. Mullarkey, Karen, date. II. Ohanian, Bernard, 1956-.
    III. Bryan, Mike.
    GV863.A1B39 1991
    796.357'0973—dc20   90-21897

Printed and bound in Italy; first printing January 1991

10 9 8 7 6 5 4 3 2 1

Previous page: Civic Stadium in Eugene, Oregon. *Photo by Robb Kendrick*

This page: The third of July at the community ball field in Westphalia,
Iowa—population 110. *Photo by David Peterson*

Baseball in America

From sandlots to stadiums,
a portrait of our national passion by 50 of today's
leading photographers

Karen Mullarkey, *Editorial Director*
Jennifer Erwitt, *Project Director*
Bill Messing, *Managing Editor*
Jennifer Barry, *Director of Design*
George Olson, *Director of Photography*
Bernard Ohanian, *Writer*
Mike Bryan, *Interviewer*

CollinsPublishersSanFrancisco
A Division of HarperCollins*Publishers*

Auburn, Alabama *Photo by Melissa Farlow*

K C Royals be...

...FIE... SCHO...

Wetmore, Kansas *Photo by Jim Richardson*

BOSTO

AT BAT -

Sherlock Holmes would have loved baseball, the source of countless mysteries. Nonsense, you say: The game is unassuming, almost innocent, played out in the open for all to see. The rules are often learned so young that they become second nature, no more mysterious than breathing. In baseball's essence, you're either safe or out, and you try to score more runs than the other team before your outs are used up. This is hardly the stuff of intrigue.

Yet the mystery is there, beginning with baseball's very birth. No one knows exactly when and where the first game was played, or who first sketched out the concept and named it baseball. Every game played since has been a whodunit in the making, a shifting constellation of events and consequences, a mix of the perfectly ordinary and the utterly surprising. And when we watch major leaguers in action, thrusting our arms skyward as we cheer, we are never really privy to what's going on in the dugouts, in discussions on the pitcher's mound, and in the minds of the players themselves.

But the most important and delightful mystery is that we love the game so—that the words "baseball" and "America" are so often paired, as in the title of this book. Young and old, player and fan, major leaguer and tee-baller, the game is us: baseball and America are a perfect match. It's just that no one has ever been able to account for the attraction.

There are those who have said that our fascination comes from a baseball game's similarity to life itself, a regular routine

occasionally punctuated by exciting and meaningful moments. There are those, like the late major league commissioner

A. Bartlett Giamatti, who have pointed to baseball's sweet sadness: "It breaks your heart," Giamatti once wrote in what

has become one of the game's most famous phrases. "It is designed to break your heart." And there are those who have

argued that baseball's timelessness, and its role as the pastoral summer game, make it the perfect sport for a 21st-century

culture that still fancies itself a 19th-century Midwestern town.

All true, perhaps, but all strangely unsatisfying as explanations. No matter. Baseball, like love and religion, should

be taken on faith; its appeal is a mystery to be savored, not solved. It is just about the very most fun you can have on a

California morning in the winter, a Minnesota afternoon in the spring, a Kentucky twilight in the summer, and a

Massachusetts evening in the fall. That's enough to make baseball our national passion—even if we can't exactly say why.

Robert Maass

The Dream Begins

Child's Play

From an interview with Charles Kuralt, CBS television commentator

I was just a fanatical fan when I was a kid in North Carolina, and for a few years in Atlanta. Nobody was nuttier than I was about baseball. For 1942 I wrote down in a notebook every single play that season: "Ray Viers popped out to shortstop." I might have missed a couple of games, but not many; I didn't want an instant of a game to pass by without my recording it.

Every chance we got, a buddy and I would ride the street car to Ponce de

Leon Park to watch the Atlanta Crackers. This was during the war, so it was a team of 4-Fs and draft rejects. But most of the players in the league were really good. One was Pete Gray, the one-armed centerfielder who played for the Memphis Chicks and then made it to the big leagues with the St. Louis Browns.

The kids in the Piedmont Park area had a team and we called ourselves the Piedmont Pirates. I played second base. For uniforms we had blue knickers and white t-shirts. My buddy found a store that sold felt letters and we had our mothers sew PIRATES on the shirts, but the letters were big and our chests small so that all you could see was the RAT. The PI and the ES were hidden in our armpits. And we didn't have anybody to play. There weren't any other teams, so we just practiced.

I still remember the feel in the hands when the bat actually, honest-to-God connected with the ball for once, and the ball headed out over the infielders. I'm sure that millions of American men—and women too, nowadays—remember that feel, especially after all those times when it stung.

Scottsbluff, Nebraska
Left: At 18 months, Mikel Huston has already learned one of baseball's basics: Keep your eye on the ball. *Photo by Bill Frakes*

Snow Hill, North Carolina
Above: "Baseball was made for kids," says Hall of Fame pitcher and former manager Bob Lemon. "Grown-ups only screw it up."
Photo by Judy Griesedieck

Michael Bryant

Anybody's Ball Game

From an interview with Peggy Noonan, author and speechwriter

Baseball is purely American because it is purely democratic, accessible to everyone. It's still affordable. It's one of the few traditions that continues to bind people in this country. Cab drivers and vice presidents can talk about the game last night, and the cab driver can top that vice president with his insights and his knowledge.

Women see baseball in more sensual terms than men see it. I like to see the faces of the guys, how hard they're concentrating; I like to see the pitcher talk to himself, the guy at the bat in his threatening stance, the concentration of the catcher (I was the catcher in junior high school). I'm watching beautiful young animals who are blessed with a concentration and a confidence and a weird commitment that fascinates me.

When I was a kid the baseball players were gods. It mattered in the history of mankind whether Mickey Mantle or Roger Maris would hit 60 home runs, and who would do it first. For some reason I don't think kids feel about Darryl Strawberry quite like I felt about Mickey Mantle and Whitey Ford. Maybe I'm wrong. But it is a changing country. I grew up in a more innocent time, when we took our heroes straight. As a kid I thought they were upstanding, gifted American men. And I really liked them.

Chicago, Illinois
Previous page: A new White Sox fan undergoes his initiation at historic Comiskey Park, now razed since the team's departure to newer quarters across the street. *Photo by Michael Bryant*

Commerce, Oklahoma
Right: The pitch sails plateward in a Saturday afternoon game on the street named for a small town's most celebrated son. *Photo by Bill Frakes*

20

Mesa, Arizona
Above: An obliging Cub signs baseballs, scorecards, and anything else fans thrust into his hands at Ho Ho Kam Park, where the Chicago team and its minor league affiliates train each spring. Mindful that collectors buy and sell their signatures for as much as $60 each, many players now sign autographs primarily at baseball card and memorabilia shows, where stars past and present command up to $20,000 for a four-hour signing spree. *Photo by Jim Mendenhall*

San Diego, California
Above right: A fan at Jack Murphy Stadium, home of the Padres, searches the field for one of his heroes. *Photo by John W. McDonough*

Oakland, California
Right: Team magazines available at most ballparks are full of statistics, names of players' wives and children, and other tidbits ranging from the useful to the impossibly arcane. *Photo by John W. McDonough*

23

Tempe, Arizona
Despite the dizzying growth in the number of adults collecting baseball cards as investments, the country's five principal baseball card companies say that 75 to 90 percent of their new sales are still to kids under 12 years of age. Thanks in part to the advent of focus groups, in which pre-teens are asked by market researchers to rate potential card designs, sales of new cards doubled in almost every year in the late 1980s and now stand at about 8 billion annually. Meanwhile, investors have transformed the sale of old cards into a $500 million enterprise—buttressed by dozens of specialized magazines and even computer programs that allow enthusiasts to keep track of their cards and chart their changes in value. *Photo by Jim Mendenhall*

Kayenta, Arizona The wind-up ... *Photo by Monty Roessel*

Auburn, Alabama ... the spectators ... *Photo by Karen Kasmauski*

Lewisville, Texas ... the lead from first ... *Photo by Brian Payne*

Auburn, Alabama ... and the post-game picture. *Photo by Karen Kasmauski*

The Best I Ever Saw

From an interview with Bill Rigney, former player and manager; Special Assistant to the General Manager, Oakland A's

When people ask who was the best player I ever saw, it's tough not to put Jackie Robinson there. Willie Mays's ability was probably the best, but the dedication of Robinson, the fire in the belly of this man, the ability to put everybody on edge made him the toughest out in the line-up. For us who played against him, black or white didn't matter. His talent bothered us more than his color, I'll tell you that. There was real animosity—no, hate is a better word—between the Giants and

Dodgers as we began to come back in 1951. A lot of bad blood. After the Dodgers beat us in Brooklyn and were 12 games ahead, we had Jackie beating on the door between the two clubhouses with his bat and yelling at our manager, Leo Durocher. He didn't like Leo. Ralph Branca was saying, "Roll out the barrel, the Giants are dead." It was ugly. We could hear all this stuff, and we just had to take it. On the field, it was war. War. But finally we tied them at the end of the season.

Then came Bobby Thomson's home run in the playoff game, and I don't think the crescendo of that homer will ever stop ringing somewhere. Not for anyone who was alive then, and a part of it. When the game was over, four Dodgers came into our clubhouse—the Duke, Pee Wee, Preacher, and Jackie. The Duke was in tears. Pee Wee said, "You kicked our butts. Keep it going." Something like that. But Jackie came in and walked all the way down to my locker and said, "I just want to tell you one thing. We didn't lose it. You won it." Then he turned around and walked out. I thought this showed the character of the man. That's why they picked Jackie Robinson to lead the black players into professional baseball.

Auburn, Alabama
Above: Allen Reaves jumps for joy as his Dixie Youth Baseball team records an out. *Photo by Karen Kasmauski*

Atlanta, Georgia
Right: A bat and ball are the stuff of laughter for five-year-old Donson Daniels. *Photo by Judy Griesedieck*

Lewisville, Texas

"To play this game well," Hall of Fame catcher Roy Campanella used to say, "you've got to have a lot of little boy in you." These days, Campy might add that it couldn't hurt to have a lot of little girl in you either, as these thirsty tee-ball players can attest. Millions of boys and girls across the country play in tee-ball leagues, which took root in the mid-1970s as an option for kids too young to hit a pitched ball—or deliver one accurately over the plate. Everyone in the line-up bats each inning, putting the soft ball in play by hitting it off a tee. *Photo by Brian Payne*

New York, New York

There had been no Little League baseball in Harlem for two decades when Iris Raiford struck a deal with her son Joshua: "I told him that if he would practice his piano," she recalls, "I'd start a league." And so she did, with about 130 players in the first year, 1989, and twice as many the next year. The league's sponsors, which include a local firehouse, a group of doctors at Harlem Hospital, and the United States Ambassador to the island nation of Vanuatu, each pony up about $800 to fund a team. Parents of participating kids are asked to contribute $25 as well to defray equipment and administrative costs but, says Raiford, "it's a Little League rule that no child be denied membership because of inability to pay."

Above, the *Sports Illustrated for Kids* team's manager, Shea Bethell, leads Anthony Espinosa, Grancis Santana, Jason Glover, and Shea-tee Bethell in calisthenics.

Raiford donates about 70 hours of her time every week during the season to administer the league, but says "it's worth everything when you see the faces of the kids"—like those of the Robert Plan Rockets (*above, right*), sharing post-game forearm bashes with parent Phillip Dunn. The league has also helped clean up Colonel Charles Young Field, located at 145th Street and Malcolm X Avenue. Adanqua McClymont of the Bowery Savings Bank Clippers may wonder how he can catch raindrops and baseballs at the same time (*right*), but rain or shine, Raiford says, "there's always a policeman walking the beat in the park when we play. One of them told me he hopes we never leave the park." *Photos by Robert Maass*

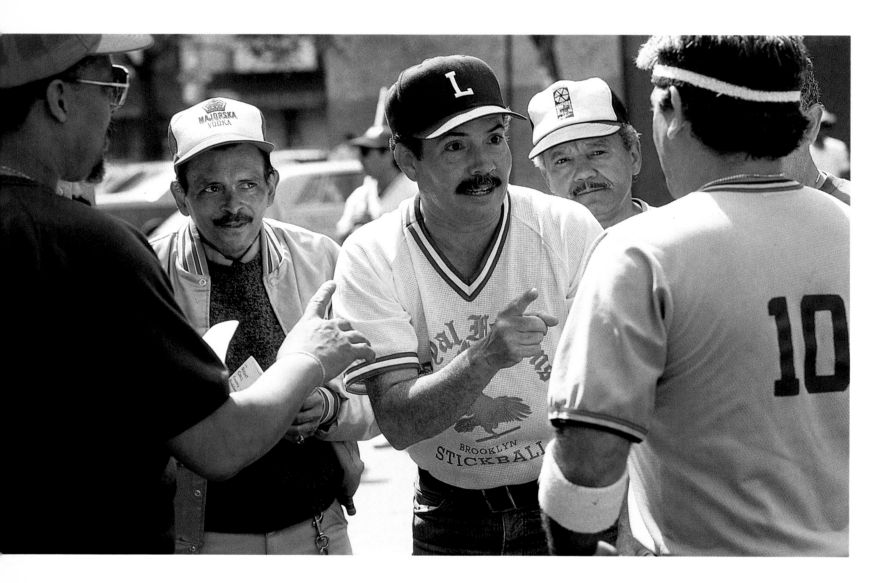

New York, New York

Above and right: The nation's largest city lost its undisputed claim as the baseball capital of the world when its beloved New York Giants and Brooklyn Dodgers headed west after the 1957 season, but its streets remain a mecca for players of stickball. Teams from Brooklyn, New Jersey, and Puerto Rico converge on Manhattan's East Harlem each Memorial Day weekend for tournament games, which are played with a spongy rubber ball that is bounced to home plate. Above, manager Pablo Perez of the Royal Falcons offers some pre-game pointers to Ralphie Rodriguez as umpire Lefty Gomez looks on. Once the seven-inning game gets under way, an opposing Minotaur batter draws a crowd with a mighty cut. It pays to make contact, because in stickball it's one strike and you're out. *Photos by Chris Maynard*

Monument Valley Tribal Park, Arizona

Following page: "I remember when I was young and had to herd sheep," says photographer Monty Roessel, who grew up here on the Navajo reservation. "My brothers and I would bring our bat, ball and gloves along so we could practice. Even years later, I knew I could find kids still doing the same thing." *Photo by Monty Roessel*

Monty Roessel

Faces of the Game (*clockwise from top left*):

Albuquerque, New Mexico
From a blind "beep baseball" batter ... *Photo by Judy Griesedieck*

San Pedro de Macoris, Dominican Republic
... to three dugout stowaways dreaming of los Estados Unidos ... *Photo by Andy Levin*

St. Paul, Minnesota
... to snowshoe baseball players in Fort Snelling State Park ... *Photo by Mitch Kezar*

Bismarck, North Dakota
... to a softballer at a 400-team extravaganza ... *Photo by John Biever*

Detroit, Michigan
... to a policeman-pitcher at a national softball tourney. *Photo by Pauline Lubens*

New York, New York Baseball parents are great for inspiring mischief ... *Photo by Robert Maass*

Des Moines, Iowa ... passing on pitching tips ... *Photo by David Peterson*

Auburn, Alabama ... comforting a pouty player ... *Photo by Karen Kasmauski*

Bradenton, Florida ... and giving last-minute pep talks. *Photo by Joe Traver*

A Chance to Grow: Baseball Camp for City Kids in Louisiana

For most kids, baseball is something to be taken for granted. All it takes is a ball and a glove to get started, and with a bat you have a game. But even those few items are out of reach for some, and with them the opportunity to learn the teamwork and fair play the game can instill. One man in Louisiana, Ron Maestri, is working to change that.

On the first day of a week-long baseball camp at the University of New Orleans, 10-year-old Anthony Gibson watches as other kids jostle for fly balls. Quiet and a bit withdrawn, Anthony stays mostly on the sidelines during the opening session of the camp, which is run by university athletic director Maestri and features a week of baseball instruction for 170 boys aged eight to thirteen who live in city housing projects. Though the camp is only in its first year, Maestri has already raised strong community support, ranging from the sheriff's department, which supplies buses to pick up the budding ballplayers each morning, to various corporate sponsors who chip in food, supplies, and cash to keep the program going. *Photo essay by David Peterson*

By the second day, a smiling Anthony has a friend in coach Maestri. "He asked me if he could be my helper," the coach says. "So I had him distribute and collect the gloves each day. He adopted me."

On the field, Anthony still has bouts of shyness, hiding his face after making an error. But he soon opens up to his fellow campers, most of whom, like him, have never had formal baseball instruction before. "I want to drive by the projects next week," Maestri muses on the camp's last day, "and see the kids playing catch." Campers who attend all five days will be awarded the balls and gloves they need to do just that.

Back home after the camp's last day, Anthony—still sporting his prized camp t-shirt along with his new glove—lofts a fly ball to a friend. The ball and glove aren't the only things Anthony has brought home: He has also won a bat, awarded to campers who showed exceptionally good sportsmanship. And Maestri's wish has come true: The grass in front of Anthony's housing project has been transformed into a playing field for a giant game of catch.

Before the camp, Ron Maestri had said, "It will all be worth it if we can reach the kids—if we can give at least one kid a dream or an experience he wouldn't have otherwise." Afterward, he reflected on Anthony Gibson: "He really blossomed during the week. And he was my buddy." Next year, says Maestri, the camp will run for two or possibly three weeks—so that dozens more Anthony Gibsons will have a chance to earn a ball, a glove, a bat, and perhaps something much more important and much more difficult to measure.

Williamsport, Pennsylvania

Early in the final game of the Little League World Series, the home-state favorites from Shippensburg are confidently counting the outs while the visitors from Tainan County, Taiwan, look on from the dugout. Some 2.5 million boys—and, since 1974, girls—play Little League baseball in 34 countries. The eight best teams of 11- and 12-year-olds gather each August at the 42-acre Little League headquarters complex in Williamsport to crown their champion. *Photos by Bill Frakes*

Williamsport, Pennsylvania

By the fourth inning of the final game, the orange-clad team from Taiwan has a safe grip on the Little League World Series. After the game, a Shippensburg player describes his team's 9-0 loss to ABC-TV's Beth Ruyak, while the victors celebrate with manager Wang Tzyy-Tsann.

Following page: Despite the loss, a young player gets to practice signing his name like a big leaguer as the Series wraps up. Some critics worry that televised games and autograph hounds give 11- and 12-year-olds an inflated view of themselves, but one veteran Little League umpire says it's the parents, not the kids, who need to grow up: "The kids often walk off the field arm in arm," he says, "while their parents won't speak to each other for a month." *Photos by Bill Frakes*

Scottsbluff, Nebraska
Corey Linnett, age nine, makes his pitch for the attention of six-year-old Kendra Portenier. *Photo by Bill Frakes*

Bill Frakes

The Road to Success

I'm Ready To Play

From an interview with Joan Jett, musician and rock star

My dad took me to a game in Baltimore on August 13, 1969. We sat behind home plate and that was the game Jim Palmer threw a no-hitter against Catfish Hunter of the Oakland A's. The first game I ever saw! Since that day baseball and the Orioles have been it for me. *It.* We lived in Maryland for five years and I went to fourteen games and they won every game.

When I watch the Orioles it would be more relaxing to be on the team. My stomach is up in my throat. When I'm on the road I call Sportsphone. Every ten minutes, too. I don't wait an hour for the game to develop. I want to know what's going on. In '83 when the Orioles were in the World Series I was on tour. I had to go on stage about the time the games were starting, so I had the road crew tell me if it was good news; bad news, don't tell me.

I'm going to fantasy camp this year. It's all I think about. January 27, in Sarasota. It's going to be the real deal on a real diamond, the uniform, the whole thing. You always wonder what it's going to be like when you get out there with a wooden bat hitting against the guys. I'd like to be the shortstop. I could play the outfield, too, but it's busier in the infield. And the way I see it, it would be easier for me, being a lefty, to turn the double play as a shortstop than as a second baseman. I've got to relax, play within myself, not show off, and really enjoy it— know what I mean? I could screw it up if I'm overanxious trying to stop the ball going through the infield.

Grosse Pointe Woods, Michigan

Left: For Dan Watkins of Grosse Pointe North High in suburban Detroit, a rally cap—devised through the twisting, turning, or mutation of a ballplayer's standard-issue wool cap—serves as an offering to the temperamental and capricious baseball gods.

Above: Watkins' teammates David Senter, Chris Meathe, Lou D'Angelo, and Scott Bernhardt engage in a round of horseplay on the bench. *Photos by Susan Biddle*

Jay Dickman

Honolulu, Hawaii

Previous page: Resplendent in pinstripes, the high-school age Buffandblus of Punahou School—who take their name from the colors of the sand and sea—sprint in the outfield before a game.

Above: The baseball expression "barreling into second base" is taken to its literal extreme on the Punahou practice field, where infielders jump over barrels rolled their way to simulate sliding runners. *Photos by Jay Dickman*

Scottsbluff, Nebraska

Above right: An inside pitch sends the batter skyward at an American Legion tournament. *Photo by Bill Frakes*

Junction City, Arkansas

Right: As the star pitcher on a small town's winning high school team—and a straight-A student to boot—Jeff Lyons has a lot to smile about. *Photo by Annie Griffiths Belt*

Moraga, California

Campolindo High School's Carey Schueler has a wicked curveball, a good slider, an average fastball, and a big psychological weapon. "Opposing batters often defeat themselves just by trying too hard," explains varsity pitching coach Dan Ward—because Carey Schueler is a girl. But the extra pressure batters put on themselves is not the main reason for Carey's success: "With her stuff," Ward says, "she's good enough to pitch for a men's team in college if she concentrates on baseball, builds up her strength, and works on her mechanics." Getting Carey to concentrate on baseball may be the hard part; although the daughter of former major league pitcher Ron Schueler has spent much of her life playing the game, she's also good enough at basketball to get scholarship offers and is a star volleyball player to boot. Still, her goal is to become the first woman to play in the major leagues. *Photo by John Storey*

Scottsbluff, Nebraska Bobbie Seibert, Mitchell Midgets. *Photo by Bill Frakes*

Oakland, California Dave Stewart, Oakland Athletics. *Photo by John Biever*

Tempe, Arizona Billy Kanwisher, Oklahoma State University. *Photo by P.F. Bentley*

Kahalu-u, Hawaii Gregg Omori, Koolau Menehunes. *Photo by Jay Dickman*

Chicago, Illinois Bob "Rapid Robert" Feller, Hall of Famer. *Photo by Michael Zagaris*

Port St. Lucie, Florida Steve Smalheiser, real estate broker. *Photo by Andy Levin*

Boston, Massachusetts Nolan Ryan, Texas Rangers. *Photo by John Biever*

Omaha, Nebraska Mike Rebhan, University of Georgia. *Photo by Rick Rickman*

Pine Bluff, Arkansas

Above: When coach Billy Bock talks, his Pine Bluff High School Zebras listen. "You never say 'if' and you never ask me 'why'," Bock tells his charges on the first day of practice each year. "You've got to have that old Zebra spirit." Bock's teams won state championships five years in a row in the 1980s, sparking *Collegiate Baseball* magazine to name him Coach of the Decade. His speech is still peppered with the colorful advice ("Don't get caught in the outhouse when the lightning strikes" is a favorite) he began giving at the start of his high school coaching career in 1964. But, he says, "Times have

changed. The kids used to work on the farm, doing chores; now they watch television on their satellite dishes." Still, Coach Bock acknowledges that there's a positive side to the new breed of high school player: "Now all the kids can get to workouts, because they all have cars."

Above right: Hitting the curve ball isn't the only thing high schoolers learn at baseball practice—much to the dismay of parents and doctors. Recent years have seen an alarming increase in the number of teenage boys, now estimated at one in four, who have tried smokeless tobacco. Congress banned television advertising of snuff and chaw soon after the U.S. Surgeon General's 1986 report linking them to cancer and gum disease, but the industry still gets plenty of TV exposure from the estimated one-third of major league players who chew.
Photos by Annie Griffiths Belt

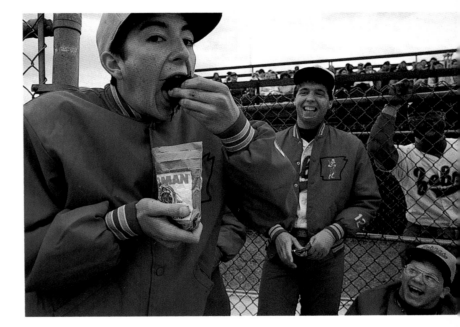

Stanford, California

Right: Advice far less colorful than Billy Bock's—but no less useful—comes from the Apple computer in the dugout at Stanford University, located in the heart of technology-rich Silicon Valley. In search of statistical tendencies that might give his team an edge, student manager Scott Schaefer uses the Macintosh to log the location, type, and outcome of every pitch during a game. *Photo by P.F. Bentley*

Scottsbluff, Nebraska

Following page: At the same ballpark where he pitched a no-hitter as an American Legion player 20 years to the day earlier, photographer Bill Frakes found young Twin Cities Zephyr Marc Gonzales sharing a laugh with Janelle Stricker, oblivious to the day's historical significance. *Photo by Bill Frakes*

Making the Move: Going Pro Out of High School in Brilliant, Ohio

After signing a contract with the Montreal Expos, 19-year-old Rick Clelland, Jr. of Brilliant, Ohio, takes a break from packing his suitcase to rerun a tape from the local news about his fifth-round selection in the June amateur baseball draft. The draft was the beginning of a hectic week as Rick—an all-state pitcher his senior year in high school—debated whether to sign with the Expos or accept a full scholarship to Auburn University in Alabama. In the end, the Expos won him over with the help of a package of bonuses valued in the range of $75,000 and immediately assigned him to their lowest-level minor league team, in Florida's Gulf Coast League. Like all the nearly 1,500 players chosen in the draft, Rick's goal is to make it to the major leagues. But the odds aren't great: Only about 3 percent of the 3,750 players in the minors make it to the big leagues in a typical year. *Photo essay by Randy Olson*

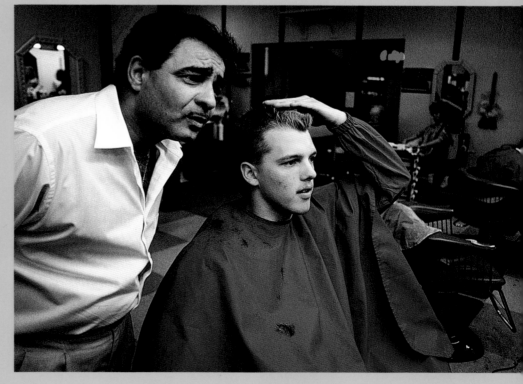

Above: After the draft, Rick and his family talk over his options with Joe Frisina, a scout with the Expos (from left: Amy Kalonick, Rick's fiancee; Rick; his sister Sheri; his mother Linda; his father Rick, Sr.; Nick Palavis, his coach from the semi-pro Palominos of Weirton, West Virginia; and Frisina). "I didn't support him signing with the Expos at first," says Amy, who's been Rick's steady since they were in seventh grade. "I liked the idea of him playing college ball. But when the scout told us how much money major league players make, I changed my mind."

Right: Before deciding to sign, Rick pitches one last game for the Palominos in their home park under the smokestacks of the Weirton Steel Company, where Rick, Sr. is a foreman. With the help of the pitching coaches in the Expo organization, who he says are the best in the business, Rick hopes to make it to the majors within five years; to hedge his bets, he plans to study at Ohio University during the off-season. His decision made, Rick stops by the family barber, Frank Luckino, for a quick trim.

Above: Rick and Amy, who picture themselves getting married when he reaches the highest level in the minor leagues, Class AAA—"two or three years from now," says Amy—take a snapshot in the final hours before he leaves for Florida.

Right: "I felt terrible when he left," says Amy, who started college as a pre-law student at Ohio University two months after Rick's departure for Florida, "but the thought of him pitching in the pros is exciting. I have pictures of him all over my dorm-room walls. He'll definitely make the majors." Rick's father is more cautious: "I say a little prayer each night to keep him healthy. All the kids at his level have talent, but if you come down with a sore arm or you pull something, it could be all over."

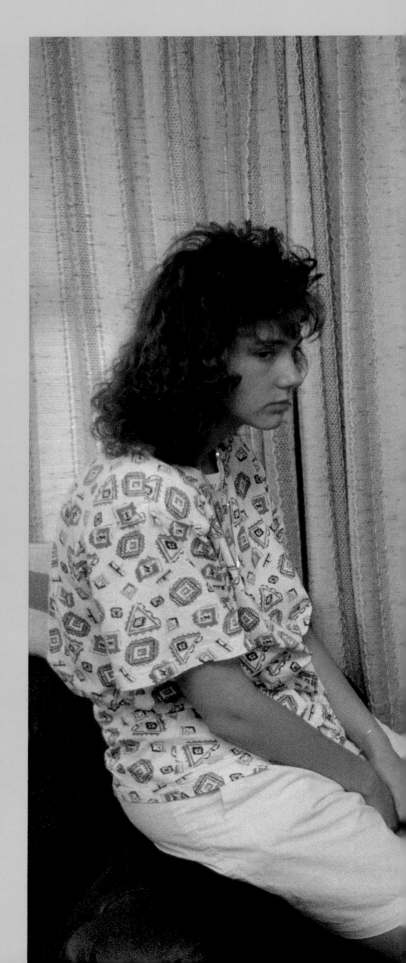

The Law of Averages

From an interview with Dick Thornburgh, Attorney General of the United States

I've been a baseball fan for five decades. I have sitting on my desk, along with my law books and books on government, the *Baseball Encyclopedia*. I have shelves full of old guides. There's something about the stats. The measure of the man in baseball is taken in fairly stark terms. Fortunately we don't rate people's character like that, but on the ballfield you're pretty naked to the observer. Occasionally you get a guy who redeems himself on a non-statistical basis, such as the smooth-fielding shortstop, but by and large the statistics are there for all to see.

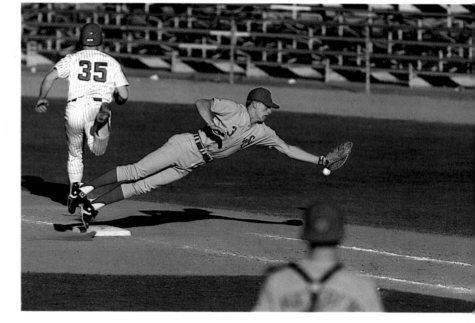

A while back I went up to Philadelphia to give a very serious speech before a civic group. The subject was the Bush administration's program for drugs and white-collar crime. After the speech we had a question-and-answer period and the questions were about the Savings and Loan scandal and other weighty matters. Finally a guy says, "Look, I understand you're some kind of baseball expert." I said, "Well, I don't know about that." The guy says, "I got a question for you. Can you name the starting line-up for the 1941 Chicago Cubs?" And I said, "Yes, I think I can. Phil Cavarretta at first base, Lou Stringer at second, Bobby Sturgeon at short, Stan Hack at third, Dom Dallessandro, Bill Nicholson and Lou Novikoff in the outfield, Clyde McCullough behind the plate, Claude Passeau and a bunch of guys I can't really remember on the mound." The guy had just happened to hit on the season I really know. It was a much better answer than any I had given about what the Bush administration was doing.

Stanford, California
Left: Stanford University's Mark Marquess, who coached the 1988 U.S. Olympic team to the gold medal in Seoul, makes his point clear during a game at the university's Sunken Diamond. *Photo by P.F. Bentley*

Tempe, Arizona
Above: Time and space coincide to ill advantage for Washington State University first baseman Rob Nichols in tournament play leading up to the College World Series. *Photo by P.F. Bentley*

Coral Gables, Florida

Above: The University of Miami finds that working as a team goes hand in hand with a winning record, which is why coach Ron Fraser insists that his Hurricanes end practice each day by running across the field in a chain. Fraser, the winningest university baseball coach in the game today, has led the Hurricanes to the College World Series 11 times. *Photo by Bill Frakes*

Telluride, Colorado

Above right: "I've never met a great player who didn't have to work harder at learning to play ball than anything else he ever did," said Ted Williams. *Photo by Eric Lars Bakke*

Orono, Maine

Right: Fordham University players stretch out before taking the field at the University of Maine. *Photo by Joe Traver*

Jeff Jacobsen

Tucson, Arizona
Previous page: Though today it's more likely made of wax than real charcoal, ballplayers still want what they call "paint" to fight off the sun's glare. University of Arizona student trainer Chris Yarter applies a dose to catcher Jack Johnson before a game with intra-state rival Arizona State University. *Photo by Jeff Jacobsen*

Honolulu, Hawaii
Below: There's no end to the rainbows as Ohio's Wright State Raiders stretch in the outfield at Rainbow Stadium before a game with the University of Hawaii Rainbows at the 15th annual Rainbow Spring Tournament. College baseball has been the main attraction for fans in Hawaii since 1987, when the Class AAA Hawaii Islanders moved to the mainland. Hawaii's weather and one of college baseball's finest facilities help lure visiting teams, so the Rainbows don't have to make many road trips. About 80 percent of the team's 60 or so games each year are played in Rainbow Stadium. *Photo by Jay Dickman*

Oklahoma City, Oklahoma

The champions and the challengers: Before the final game of the 1990 College World Series in women's softball, Karla Parent of the five-time champion UCLA Bruins calmly braids teammate Kelly Inouye's hair in the dugout, while the Fresno State Bulldogs—in search of the title that has eluded them on three other trips to the finals—intently watch UCLA batting practice. *Photos by Judy Griesedieck*

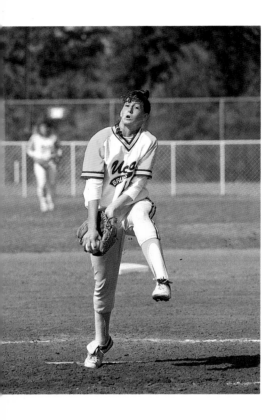

Oklahoma City, Oklahoma

Above and right: Nineteen-year-old pitcher Heather Compton shows off the game face and whipsaw delivery that enabled her to pop Fresno State's bubble with a 2-0 shutout in the final game of the College World Series. Compton is one of 12 athletes each year to win women's softball scholarships to UCLA. More than 500 four-year colleges and universities sponsor women's softball teams. *Photos by Judy Griesedieck*

Washington, D.C.

Following page: Julie Croteau mixes it up with the boys as first basewoman for Maryland's St. Mary's College. Croteau, or "J.C." to her teammates, is the first woman to see substantial playing time with a college baseball team, and the first to hit safely. Spiritually, she is the daughter of the pioneering women of the All-American Girls Professional Baseball League. Members of the 10 teams in the league—founded by Chicago Cubs owner Philip K. Wrigley—played their hardball in skirts and high socks for 12 years before the enterprise went out of business in 1954. "If there were a women's league to-day," says Croteau, "I'm sure I'd be in it. But it's hard for me to think about playing with women, because I've been playing with men all my life." *Photo by Pete Souza*

Pete Souza

Austin, Texas

The stakes are high for the six teams gathered in the Texan capital for the NCAA Central Regional Tournament: The winner earns a trip to the College World Series in Omaha. And for Creighton University, a berth in the World Series would mean a chance to play before the home folks. Pitcher Dan Smith of the Creighton Bluejays calls on his rally cap for luck (*left*) as he watches a teammate take a headfirst dive (*above*). *Photos by Jay Dickman*

Austin, Texas

It's long been said that the two most popular sports in the Lone Star State are football and spring football, but come NCAA baseball playoff time, University of Texas Longhorns fans swear by their team. The players salute their followers with the traditional "Hook 'em Horns" gesture (*right*), but it's not enough to keep Cal State Fullerton from winning the regional and advancing to Omaha. *Photos by Jay Dickman*

Omaha, Nebraska

Terry Childers seals off home plate in a key play at the College World Series. The University of Georgia catcher holds the ball wrapped tightly in his mitt, despite the football-like efforts of Oklahoma State University's Brian Kelly to jar it loose and score the tying run in the seventh inning of the final game. Two innings later, Childers and his teammates mob pitcher Dave Fleming, who preserved the 2-1 lead to bring his team its first-ever national baseball championship. The 1980s saw a marked increase in both the popularity and level of play of college baseball; the colleges have become a serious training ground for potential major leaguers as the number of minor league teams has decreased. More than 135,000 fans attended the 14-game, 8-team competition in 1990, setting an all-time College World Series attendance record. *Photos by Rick Rickman*

Reaching for the Top

Oneonta, New York

Above: Even as they move into the house they'll share with two other young minor leaguers, Oneonta Yankees Sam Militello, Ron Frazier, and Darren Hodges are focused on moving up—toward the major leagues and away from Class A ball.

Following page: The day before the season opener, Oneonta pitchers Kirt Ojala and Todd Malone listen to tips from coach Mark Shiflett. It must have been good advice: Both pitchers struck out more than one batter an inning over the course of the season, and between them they won ten games and lost only two. *Photos by Bradley Clift*

Tampa, Florida

Right: Jovino Carvajal of the Dominican Republic reflects on life at the New York Yankees' minor league training complex; out on the field, Carl Everett, the team's number one choice in the June draft, grits his teeth as the team runs wind sprints. *Photos by Bradley Clift*

Bradley Clift

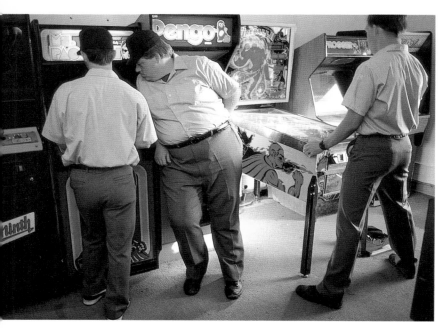

Daytona Beach, Florida
Pat Kendrick and his fellow students at the Wendelstedt
Umpire School practice the correct stance for calling balls and
strikes (*above*). The top fifth of the students are invited to an
evaluation course sponsored by the major leagues, where each
has a one-in-two chance of being signed to a contract at the
lowest minor league level. There they'll earn about $2,300 per
month while making a slow climb to the majors, which takes an
average of seven years. After a long day of classroom time and
on-field workouts, Tony Hendrix (*above, left*) steals a quiet
moment in the practice-field bathroom. *Photos by Randy Olson*

Cocoa Beach, Florida
At another school, run by Joe Brinkman and Bruce Froemming,
students avoid an arcade game with a baseball theme during a
break in the day's activities (*left*). *Photo by Randy Olson*

San Pedro de Macorís, Dominican Republic

Looking for a leg up in the baseball world, local teenagers get loose before a workout at the San Francisco Giants compound in a city whose name has become synonymous with baseball. Sixteen players from San Pedro de Macorís, a city of about 100,000 people, were on major league spring training rosters in 1990, as were dozens more from elsewhere in the Dominican Republic. One of the proudest occasions in the nation's history came on April 27, 1986, when nine different Dominicans played shortstop in the major leagues on the same day.

El beisbol was introduced to the Dominican Republic by U.S. Marines who occupied the small Caribbean nation from 1916 to 1924. In 1956, nine years after the breaking of the major league color barrier, Osvaldo José Virgil y Pichardo—better known to baseball fans as Ozzie Virgil, Sr.—made his debut with the New York Giants, becoming the first Dominican to play in the big leagues. Increasingly since then, baseball has, along with its other attractions, been seen as a way to escape the poverty of a country where annual income averages $1,200.

Several major league teams hold regular tryout camps in the Dominican Republic, and some—like the Giants—maintain group housing facilities or baseball "academies" at which, under Dominican law, players can be housed and evaluated for a maximum of 30 days before being either signed to a contract or released. *Photo by Andy Levin*

Andy Levin

Campo las Palmas, Dominican Republic
Previous page: "Baseball is like a religion here," says Ralph
Avila, the chief Dominican scout for the Los Angeles Dodgers.
Photo by Andy Levin

San Pedro de Macorís, Dominican Republic
Above and right: "In the Dominican Republic," says shortstop
Alfredo Griffin, whose career has included successful stints with
the Cleveland Indians, Toronto Blue Jays, Oakland A's, and Los
Angeles Dodgers, "there are only two things to do. You either
work in a sugar mill or play baseball." The choice is an easy one
for a group of boys outside Tetelo Vargas Stadium, named for a
Dominican legend who, though he never played in the United
States, led the Dominican League in hitting at the age of 50.
Nearby (*right*), another boy practices his own sweet swing, perhaps inspired by the major leaguers who return home each winter
to work with young players.

Following page: Players at the Giants camp hope for their day
in the sun as they line up for a tryout. *Photos by Andy Levin*

Andy Levin

Bradenton, Florida
Left: Their day of practice and classroom strategy sessions over, young players at the Pittsburgh Pirates minor league spring training camp hit the phones to check that everyone is safe at home.
Photo by Joe Traver

Near Dillon, Montana
Following page: The minor leagues are notorious for long bus rides, and none is longer than the 17-hour trip the Pioneer League's Salt Lake Trappers make to Canada to play the Medicine Hat Blue Jays in eastern Alberta. Until they reach Class AAA, the last stop before the majors, these young players won't know the joys of traveling to games by plane—where they'll find that sleeping in the overhead compartments is generally frowned upon.
Photo by Rick Rickman

Rick Rickman

Orono, Maine
Above left: A pair of groundskeepers lay it on the line before a game at the University of Maine's annual tournament. *Photo by Joe Traver*

Durham, North Carolina
Left: With the infield safely covered in case of rain, it's time for some impromptu roll playing for members of the grounds crew at Durham Athletic Park, home of the the Bulls—one of the most successful franchises in the minor leagues. The team, which plays in the Carolina League, routinely leads all other Class A organizations in attendance. *Photo by Andy Levin*

Gastonia, North Carolina
Above: Using a lawnmower is an act of optimism in some parts of Sims Legion Field, home of the Gastonia Rangers of the Class A South Atlantic League. *Photo by David Burnett*

Pompano Beach, Florida
The dog days last nearly all summer long on Florida's southeast coast, where the Class A Miracle play their home games. The team's mascot, Jericho the Wonder Dog, picks up stray balls and puts them in his basket, which he also uses to carry refreshment to the umpires between innings. The daily ritual at Pompano Municipal Stadium is the brainchild of team president Mike Veeck, who comes by his zaniness honestly: His father, the late Bill Veeck, owned and operated several promotion-happy major league teams. The elder Veeck is credited with pioneering the use of flashy scoreboard graphics and dreaming up the idea of giveaway nights, in which fans get free bats, tote bags, hats, and other goodies—usually supplied by sponsors—simply for attending a ballgame. In a famous incident in 1951, he tested the limits of the sport on several counts by sending 3'7" Eddie Gaedel to bat in a major league game, on the theory that no pitcher could strike him out. Gaedel walked. *Photos by Bill Frakes*

Pride of the Pitcher's Mound

From an interview with Charley Pride, country musician and former minor league player

I was the first pitcher in 16 tries to beat the Willie Mays All-Stars. I'm the proud one who held them 4-2 in Victoria, Texas. Four innings of shutout ball, 1956. I was a knuckleballing sonofagun who had one of the finest you've ever seen. That was after I cracked my elbow. Prior to that I had all three: the hummer, the hook, and the change. Certain games I used to laugh at the hitters coming up, thinking they could hit me.

The night I beat the All-Stars I got up and sang at a local club in Victoria. I was always singing. I'd sing on the bus. People told me I'd make more money singing than I would playing baseball, at a hundred dollars a month and two dollars a day eating money. But I said I wanted to go to the majors and break all the records by the time I was 35, and then I'd go into singing. That was my plan, but it didn't work out. It eluded me.

In '62 I went out to the Angels but my arm got sorer and sorer. It was too early in the season. Marv Grissom was the pitching coach and he said, "Charley, you don't have a major league arm, we don't believe. We're going to send you home." I said, "Don't do that, please. I'll pay my own way to stay here. In time it'll come around." But I ended up back in Montana. Then they ran over my foot with a slag truck at the smelter where I worked. I've got a screw in there. I believe if I hadn't done that, when I lost a year, I might have made it.

Nuevo Laredo, Mexico
It's opening night for Los Tecolotes de los Dos Laredos, a Mexican League team that divides its home schedule between Nuevo Laredo and its sister city of Laredo, Texas. The Tecos, or Owls, compete in the Mexican League against teams sporting such names as the Saltillo Sarape Makers, the Union Laguna Cotton Pickers, and the San Luis Potosí Cactus Men. *Photo by Ethan Hoffman*

Salt Lake City, Utah

Fowl ball is the drawing card at Derks Field, where a crowd of more than 8,000 fans watches the Famous Chicken clown around just off the first-base line during a Pioneer League game between the home-town Trappers and the Medicine Hat Blue Jays. The Chicken, whose real name is Ted Giannoulas, began his career at San Diego radio station KGB in 1974 for what he calls the "poultry sum" of $2 per hour. Now, the Chicken performs some 250 times a year—including about 100 professional baseball games—at better than $5,000 a night. *Photo by Rick Rickman*

The Bronx, New York "Why do I like baseball?" asks Yogi Berra ... *Photo by Andy Levin*

Bismarck, North Dakota "... Because it's fun to play! ... *Photo by P.F. Bentley*

Yosemite National Park, California "... Without baseball ... *Photo by Dan Warsinger*

New York, New York "... I would have had to go to work somewhere." *Photo by Chris Maynard*

San Francisco, California
Proving that baseball equipment is where you find it, broom-wielding Tony Guzman strides into a pitched ball of masking tape delivered by fellow Alaska Airlines employee Kevin Barron on the tarmac at San Francisco International Airport. *Photo by George Olson*

Oahu, Hawaii and Weehawken, New Jersey Diamonds in the rough, from sugar cane fields to the Lincoln Tunnel. *Photos by Rich Clarkson*

Down Home Heroes: Surviving the Low Minors in Appalachia

Baseball announcers often talk about players who can hit the ball a country mile, but a significantly shorter shot can reach the property of the Sheets family of Pulaski, Virginia. Less than 100 feet separates the right-field wall of Calfee Park from Patricia Sheets's clothesline (*left*), and foul balls occasionally hit the family house when the Braves—the local representatives in the Appalachian League—are playing at home. But the proximity of the ballpark means that the Sheetses and their neighbors can watch professional baseball from their front porch in the shadow of the Blue Ridge Mountains, and hope that one or two of the Appalachian League players they've come to admire will make it to the major leagues someday. *Photo essay by Joe McNally*

Having arrived at the ballpark up to four hours before the first pitch at 7:00 p.m., Trent Mongero, Barry Chiles, Mike Place, and Armando Rodriguez of the Braves have plenty of time for pre-game chores. The Appalachian League, like the Pioneer and Gulf Coast leagues, is a rookie league—putting it at the very bottom of the minor league ladder. Players earn between $850 and $1000 a month for the 10-week season, with $11 a day for meals while on the road. The rest of the year, rookie league players return home to concentrate on keeping in shape while attending college, driving delivery trucks, or working in health clubs.

While it can be hard for Appalachian League players to make ends meet, and the locker rooms are less than luxurious (*right*), the price is right for fans. Space for lawn chairs on the general-admission terrace overlooking the third-base line at DeVault Memorial Stadium in Bristol, Virginia goes for $25 for a package of 30 games featuring the hometown Tigers (*above, right*).

When pitcher Tom Benson and catcher Matt Brown find the sticky Southern nights too much to handle (*top*), they can console themselves by remembering that major league stars Kirby Puckett, Kent Hrbek, and Gary Gaetti all once wore the uniform of the Twins of Elizabethton, Tennessee. Life with the Twins means enduring long bus rides to small towns in Virginia, North Carolina, and West Virginia, and usually playing home games before fewer than 500 fans—many of whom risk broken windshields by parking just beyond the right-field fence at Joe O'Brien Field (*right*).

Back in Pulaski, it doesn't take long for Linda Edwards and Nannatta Burton to tally up the night's receipts (*above*). Ticket prices for Braves games range from $1.50 to $3; hot dogs, large sodas, popcorn and nachos all cost $1. At Calfee Field, as in most of the Appalachian League, beer sales are prohibited by city ordinance.

Following page: The game with West Virginia's Princeton Patriots over, the dugout that is the Twins' home—part living room, part office, part repository of improbable futures—waits for another day. The Twins will return at 3:00 p.m.

Joe McNally

Ronald C. Modra

The Major Leagues

Detroit, Michigan

Above left: The groundskeepers at historic Tiger Stadium chalk out the batter's boxes before a game with the Chicago White Sox. *Photo by Richard Marshall*

Flushing, New York

Left: "The dirt," says longtime groundskeeper Roger Bossard, "is the most important part of a professional baseball field. That's where 70 percent of the game is played." Head groundskeepers supervise employees like the men dragging the infield at Shea Stadium, and work about 100 hours a week when the home team is in town. *Photo by Nicole Bengiveno*

Cincinnati, Ohio

Above: The grounds crew at Riverfront Stadium, one of 10 major league parks with artificial turf instead of grass, covers the playing field before a rainstorm. *Photo by Judy Griesedieck*

A Fan for All Seasons

From an interview with Braves fan Pearl Sandow, Hall of Fame honoree

I'll have you know I'm in the new museum at Cooperstown, as a statue. Until this year I hadn't missed a Braves game for 24 years, since they came here in 1966. Then I fell and broke both shoulders. It was just a horrible accident. They tell me the first thing I said when I was conscious was, "Will I be ready for the baseball season?" Of course I wasn't but I'm fortunate to be alive, so I quit worrying about it. I'll just start another string.

I'm 78 years old. They gave me a lifetime pass in 1975 but I still buy the seat next to me. That's what I call my junk seat. Everybody comes by and chats. I worked for the government before I retired and if we had day games I just took leave time and went as part of my vacation. For years I didn't realize I hadn't missed any games. I just knew I went every day. Everybody says, "You're the funniest person. You don't yell, you don't fuss." I say, "Look, I'm enjoying the ball *game*."

I've seen so many of them come here as youngsters. Little Jerry Royster was always a favorite; he came as such a young man and left 11 years later as a mature person. And Eddie Mathews with the Crackers, throwing the ball up into the stands as much as he did on the field. I get Christmas cards from them now, and pictures of their children, and now pictures of their grandchildren. They've been so faithful. When Dale Murphy got traded to Philadelphia he called me up to say goodbye. That just broke my heart but I feel much better knowing he's building a home here. He'll be coming back.

Cincinnati, Ohio
Faithful fans of the Cincinnati Reds brave blustery weather to watch the city's annual opening-day parade. *Photo by Andy Levin*

Chicago, Illinois *Photo by Ronald C. Modra*

AT BAT   BALL   STRIKE   OUT

VISITORS   INNING

CUBS

Chicago, Illinois *Photo by Ronald C. Modra*

Working the Game: Major League Umpires on the Road

In the relative tranquility of their locker room at Yankee Stadium in the Bronx, American League umpires Drew Coble and Tim Welke steal a few minutes before a night game to play cribbage. But once they take the field, they'll have to put all thoughts of winning and losing aside.

Umpires work in crews of four. Except for two weeks of vacation time, members of a crew get together every day during the course of the 162-game season. Salaries start at $50,000 in the majors, with top umps making as much as $120,000 annually. But virtually to a man, they remain unhappy about a grueling travel schedule that, despite its first-class flights and $170 daily allowance for meals and hotels, keeps them continually on the road—hopping from plane to cab to hotel to stadium and back again, never spending more than four days in a row in any one city. To kill time in the off hours, the umps take in matinees, hit the golf course, visit friends, and rack up huge long-distance phone bills talking to their families. Then, 90 minutes before the first pitch, it's time to suit up at the ballpark. *Photo essay by Andy Levin*

As game time nears, Dale Ford, a two-sport man who spends the off-season officiating college basketball, has his first close shave of the night (*above, left*). Plate umpire and crew chief Jim Evans rubs a special mud—gathered in secret from the bottom of the Delaware River—on the night's 5 dozen game balls so that pitchers can get a better grip on them (*left*). Evans, who operates an umpiring school in Arizona and authors a baseball-rule comic strip, says he loves what he does so much that "when friends take me to their kids' Little League games, I root for the umps."

Coble, Welke, Evans, and Ford stand at attention for the national anthem at a game between the Indians and the Toronto Blue Jays in Cleveland (*above*). Toronto's Dave Steib will throw a no-hitter in the game, but Evans leaves the excitement to the crowd in the stands. "I'm a fan of baseball," he says, "but I'm not a fan of the game I'm working. In fact, the first time I worked a no-hitter I didn't know it until someone told me after the game."

Phantoms of the Ballyard

From an interview with Bill James, author, The Bill James Baseball Abstract

Baseball is a wonderful form of education. The ways we have of learning about baseball are better than our ways of learning about anything else. A young child can acquire knowledge about baseball from television, radio, newspapers, books. The game is open to you if you're a poet or an accountant, if you're a left-brain or a right-brain person. Nothing else in this country does so good a job of teaching the public about itself. I go to games, I listen to games on the radio, I watch some on TV, I check the box scores every morning, I have fantasy teams, I read books. The game is everywhere. Following another sport like that is possible, but it's a lot of work. That's one reason people are into baseball. But the green grass and the blue skies are wonderful, too. An athlete can love basketball as much as he loves baseball—but can a poet?

I have this idea that everybody who plays baseball well enough to stay in the majors for 10 or 15 years changes the game in some way, so when he leaves the game he remains behind on the field. If you really understood baseball history you could see in every game the image of everybody who's ever played really well. How did Ernie Banks change the game? He was the first guy to use the whip-handle bat. Keith Hernandez? He was the first player in 60 years to front the runner at first base in just the way he did. George Brett? When you see a player go to the plate with a line of pine tar on his bat that stops abruptly, you're seeing George Brett. That's my basic fascination with baseball right now: trying to learn its history well enough that I can see in each moment of the game all the people who've played the game. Quite a job. It has no end.

Boston, Massachusetts
Left: Nolan Ryan of the Texas Rangers, who has struck out more batters and thrown more no-hitters than any pitcher in baseball history, tucks into the wind-up. *Photo by John Biever*

Flushing, New York
Above: San Francisco Giants right fielder Mike Kingery comes up short in a leaping bid for a ball hit by Darryl Strawberry. *Photo by Chuck Solomon*

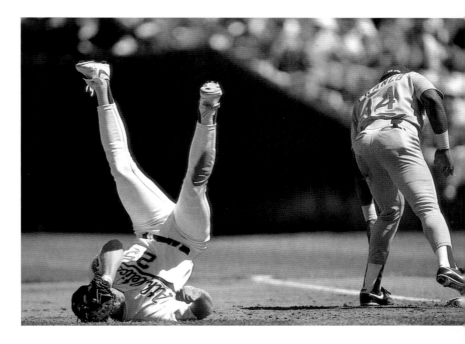

Flushing, New York

Previous page: "Yer outta there!" Emphatic ump Eric Gregg delivers the bad news to Matt Williams of the San Francisco Giants as New York Mets catcher Charlie O'Brien, ball in mitt, scans the infield to see if another throw is in order.

Left: His eyes shielded from the glare of the late summer sun and his uniform streaked with infield dirt, San Francisco Giants first baseman Will "The Thrill" Clark follows the flight of the ball as he heads for first base in a game against the New York Mets at Shea Stadium. The swaggering Clark, whom Giants teammate Terry Kennedy calls "the best baseball player I've ever seen," has been a star ever since his first major league at-bat—a 1986 home run off pitcher Nolan Ryan. *Photos by Chuck Solomon*

Oakland, California

Above: Oakland A's first baseman Mark McGwire takes a tumble while Julio Franco of the Texas Rangers returns safely to the bag.

Following page: McGwire keeps another Texas runner on his toes. *Photos by John W. McDonough*

John W. McDonough

St. Louis, Missouri
Above left: Friends decked out in Cardinal red share a laugh at Busch Stadium, home of one of baseball's most storied teams. *Photo by Richard Marshall*

Chicago, Illinois
Left: The Cubs flag flies atop Wrigley Field on the city's North Side. *Photo by Ronald C. Modra*

The Bronx, New York
Above: In the bleachers at Yankee Stadium, a fan is a fan forever. Throughout the major leagues, attendance has reached all-time highs in recent years, with the 26 teams averaging more than 2 million paying customers each—nearly double the 1970 figure. And why not? Adjusted for inflation, ticket prices to major league games in the 1980s were as low as in 1920. *Photo by Andy Levin*

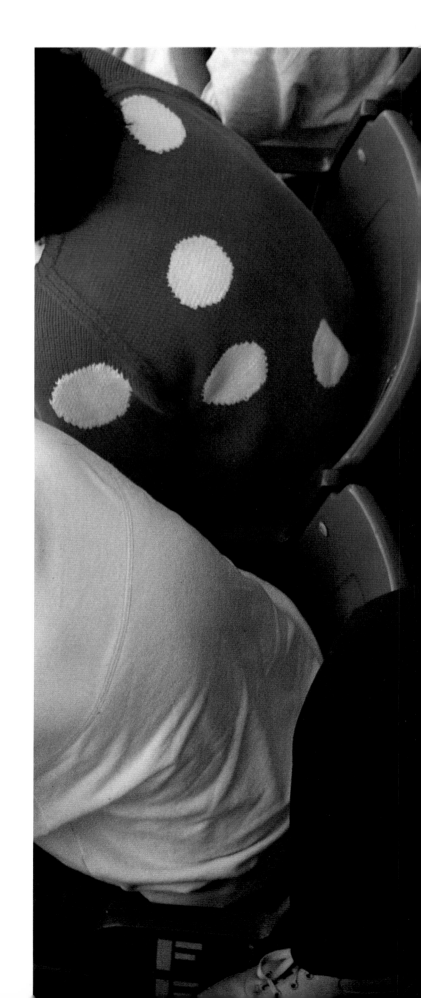

Omaha, Nebraska

Top: Hot dog! What would a day at the ballpark be without one?
Photo by Rick Rickman

Arlington, Texas

Above: True to their geography—where the melting of cultures has
given rise to the term "Tex-Mex"—Rangers concessionaires sell
nachos with cheese at each game at Texas Stadium in the suburbs
of Dallas. *Photo by Patrick Tehan*

Los Angeles, California

Right: At Dodger Stadium, as throughout the major leagues, you
can still buy your peanuts and Cracker Jacks. But you can also dine
on tofu hot dogs on whole wheat buns (Candlestick Park, San Francisco), sushi (Anaheim Stadium), knishes (Yankee Stadium), brat-
wurst (County Stadium, Milwaukee), Texas barbecue sandwiches
(the Astrodome, Houston), and Big Macs (the SkyDome, Toronto).
And in the international city of Montreal, visitors to Olympic
Stadium—or Le Stade Olympique—can choose among chow mein,
egg rolls, spare ribs, pineapple chicken, pizza, tacos, souvlaki, Greek
salad, smoked meat sandwiches, and hamburgers from Burger King.
Photo by Patrick Tehan

Chicago, Illinois

Mr. Wrigley's neighborhood: Fans pay as much as $20 to sit on rooftops near the ballpark to watch the Cubs play (*above*), although most tenants get free "roof rights" in the buildings where they live. In some apartments here in Wrigleyville, including one estimated to lie 455 feet from home plate (*above, right*), there's no need to head for the roof: The view from the living room window is good enough. For those hoping to catch a home run without paying the price of admission, the place to be is Waveland Avenue (*right*). *Photos by Randy Olson*

Flushing, New York

Following page: Precipitation is the mother of invention for these fans, who use a variety of methods—including promotional gym bags given to them as they entered the ballpark—to ward off the rain at Shea Stadium. *Photo by Misha Erwitt*

Misha Erwitt

Port St. Lucie, Florida

Fantasies of the body: "I can't explain the feeling when you first see the uniform with your name on the back," says Fred Schwartz, showing off his stance for his camera-toting son at a New York Mets fantasy camp. "I'd be crazy not to go." Schwartz, an attorney from Long Island, pays about $3,500 each year to dress up like a Met and spend a winter week at the team's spring training facility, where ordinary Joes and Janes rub shoulders with former major leaguers. The week culminates as campers—including Mark Claxton, Nancy Hamm, Bill Bufton, Robert Aldrich, and Robert Quast (*above, right*)—play a game against their heroes of old. The annual contest has provided regular camper Schwartz with one of his most cherished mementos: a ball signed by master pitcher Tom Seaver, who struck Schwartz out and then signed the ball, "To Fred, take 3 and sit down, Tom Seaver." *Photos by Andy Levin*

New York, New York

Fantasies of the mind: The players are real but the teams are not in the league that spawned a national craze. In a Rotisserie league, which takes its name from the now-defunct New York restaurant where the idea was hatched in 1981, participants—or "owners"—draw teams from a list of all active major league players. The owner whose players have the best combination of individual statistics at season's end wins a cash prize, usually taken from the money each has put in at the beginning of the season to "buy" his or her particular line-up. More than 500,000 owners, usually in groups of 10 or 12 friends or colleagues, now take part in the phenomenon. The founders of the first league (*right*), many of whom are magazine writers and book editors, sit in the exact same chairs in the exact same room every year to bid on players. *Photo by Chris Maynard*

Oakland, California

Muscular outfielder Jose Canseco—his uniform sporting the elephant that was the Athletics' symbol in Philadelphia and Kansas City for decades before their arrival in Oakland—gets a hand from a fan before a Labor Day weekend game with the Texas Rangers. While Canseco's matinee-idol looks and penchant for fast cars account for much of the attention thrown his way, baseball people agree that he fits the classic five-part definition of a superstar: He can hit for average, hit for power, run, throw, and field. *Photo by John W. McDonough*

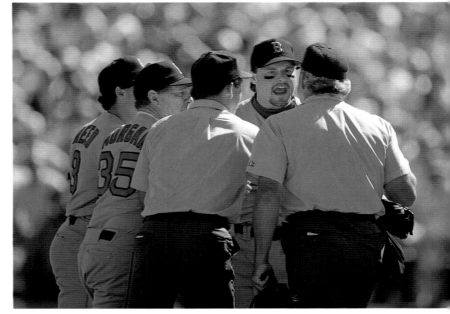

Oakland, California

With Athletics like Terry Steinbach running past catcher Tony Peña and the Red Sox at every turn in the American League Championship Series (*above*), Boston manager Joe Morgan is the picture of exasperation (*above, right*).

Star pitcher Roger Clemens (*right*) has to be restrained by Morgan and teammate Jody Reed after being kicked out of the final game for describing home plate umpire Terry Cooney in less than flattering terms. *Photos by Heinz Kluetmeier*

Oakland, California
Cincinnati Reds pitcher Jose Rijo takes the happiest shower of them all, moments after being named Most Valuable Player in the World Series. Rijo, the son-in-law of Hall of Fame pitcher Juan Marichal, became the first Dominican player ever to win the coveted honor of World Series MVP. *Photo by Heinz Kluetmeier*

Telling the Story: An Ohio Sportswriter Follows the Reds

Hal McCoy considers himself one of the luckiest guys in America: "I love to travel, I love to write, and I love baseball," says the 49-year-old sportswriter for the *Dayton Daily News*, "and I get paid for all of it." McCoy has covered the Cincinnati Reds since 1972, arriving at the ballpark three to four hours before game time each day. By the time the game is about to start, McCoy is at his place in the press box (*right*), scorebook within arm's reach as he transcribes quotes from his pregame interviews for the game story and his four-times-a-week column. Because his deadline for the paper's earliest edition is usually about 15 minutes after the game ends, McCoy writes a running story during the game, leaving just enough time after the last pitch for a few finishing touches before transmitting his work from his laptop computer to his editors in Dayton. He prides himself on not missing an inning during the baseball season: "I work straight through from spring training to the World Series," he says, "without a day off. I never get bored, because every game is different."

Photo essay by Judy Griesedieck

As part of his pre-game routine, McCoy interviews players such as rookie first baseman Hal Morris (*above, right*) and Reds manager Lou Piniella (*above*) in the clubhouse, in the dugout, and on the field. "Players are more difficult to deal with since big money came into the game," he says. "They're more thin-skinned. The Big Red Machine of the mid-1970s were the last guys who wanted to sit around to talk about baseball with the press. Today's players figure they don't need the publicity." After the game, McCoy rushes down to the clubhouse to get reactions from the team to flesh out the game story for his paper's second edition, which he has until midnight to file. "I plan to do this until I retire," he says while scribbling down notes and standing on a ledge in a stuffy locker room (*right*). "I don't even think of it as work."

Like many baseball people in southern Ohio, McCoy traces both the biggest thrill and the saddest moment of his career to the same man—former Reds player and manager Pete Rose, a Cincinnati native whose name graces the street outside Riverfront Stadium. Rose was banned from baseball in 1989 for gambling and later imprisoned for tax evasion. "When Pete passed Ty Cobb on the all-time hit list in 1985, it was the only time I ever saw people in the press box stand up and cheer," McCoy says. "But later, I broke the story that baseball officials were investigating him for gambling. Personally I felt very sad about doing it, but professionally I was proud."

Philadelphia, Pennsylvania

Left: Although he's banned from active participation in organized baseball, Pete Rose still shows up at the ballpark from time to time: At ceremonies honoring retired Phillies star Mike Schmidt, for instance, Rose's recollections of his former teammate are shown on the scoreboard at Veterans Stadium. Schmidt is considered a shoo-in for election to the Hall of Fame in Cooperstown, New York. While Rose's statistics certainly argue for his election as well, many of the baseball writers who make up the Hall of Fame electorate are likely to shun him because of his involvement with gamblers. *Photo by Michael Bryant*

Port Charlotte, Florida

Above: Sore muscles aren't the only things that need limbering up at spring training: Ballplayers and reporters alike have to get back in the groove of the pre-game interview. Above, Carolyn Burns of ESPN visits with Nolan Ryan of the Texas Rangers. *Photo by Caryn Levy*

Chicago, Illinois

"Say it ain't so": Sitting outside Comiskey Park before the last game ever played there, Jeff Weingartner and Jeff Beaudry (*above, left*) bring to mind the little boy who made those four words a permanent part of baseball's language. White Sox star Joe Jackson became the object of the boy's plea after he and several of his teammates were banned from baseball for conspiring to throw the 1919 World Series. *Photo by Michael Bryant*

Left: The paint was chipping off the old seats—some of which had survived two different numbering systems—but the oldest ballpark in the majors, hailed as The Baseball Palace of the World when it opened in 1910, was loved throughout baseball for its history and character, right down to the posts that forced some fans to twist and crane their necks to see the field. *Photo by Bill Smith*

Above: Even before the old stadium succumbed to the wreck-
ing ball, the new Comiskey Park—billed as a happy marriage
of old Comiskey's charm and the creature comforts of a modern ballpark—was rising across the street (*above*). But one
feature of the new ballpark may be jarring to baseball purists:
a private club with, according to the White Sox front office,
"private phone booths, coat/briefcase checking, and fax ma-
chines." Say it ain't so! *Photo by Bill Smith*

Caryn Levy

The Game Endures

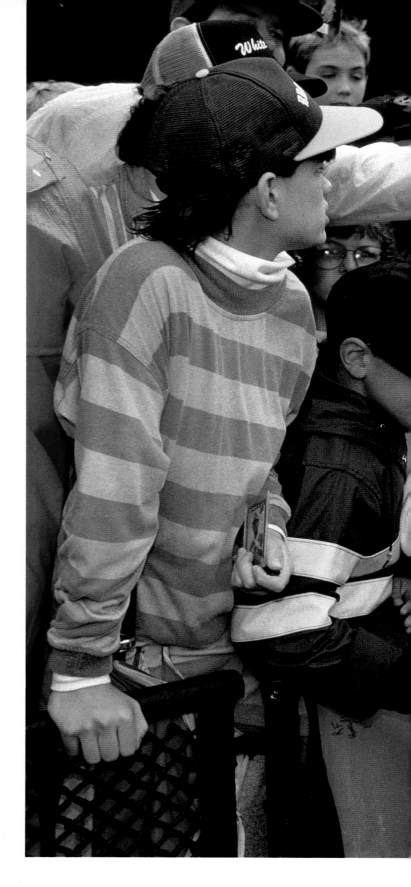

Baxter Springs, Kansas

Above left: "If you play well and know what to do on the field," says Calvin Mishler as he works with Travis Sills on his fielding form, "you've won, regardless of the score." Mishler has been building winners out of young men since 1955 as the coach, each and every year, of the same Baxter Springs Little League team, Youngman Construction. "Why do I do it?" he asks. "Because a man once took the time with me to teach me the game. I wouldn't swap places with anyone." *Photo by Bill Frakes*

Seattle, Washington

Left: While many of his contemporaries were playing in old-timers' games, Ken Griffey experienced what he described as "the best thing that's ever happened to me" on August 31, 1990. That evening, the 40-year-old Griffey, a three-time All-Star best known as a member of Cincinnati's Big Red Machine in the 1970s, made baseball history by playing left field for the Seattle Mariners while his son, Ken Griffey, Jr., played in center. Each hit a single in the first inning, prompting Junior to say, "When I saw him get that hit, I wanted to cry. He'll always be the best to me." Six weeks after celebrating the 5-2 victory with a post-game

hug, father and son enhanced their legend by hitting back-to-
back home runs against the Angels in Anaheim. Dozens of sons
have followed their fathers into the major leagues over the years,
but the Griffeys were the first to play in the same game. *Photo by
Harley Soltes*

Baltimore, Maryland

Above: The warm embrace of the Griffeys would have been
impossible on a major league field before 1947, when Jackie
Robinson of the Brooklyn Dodgers became the first black major
leaguer in baseball's modern era. Before then, black stars such as
Bob Harvey, shown signing autographs at an old-timers' contest
before an Orioles game at Municipal Stadium, were forced to do
their swinging and sliding in the Negro Leagues on teams such
as the Birmingham Black Barons, the Baltimore Elite Giants,
and the Kansas City Monarchs. Baseball fans can only wonder
how black stars like Josh Gibson, Piper Davis, and Cool Papa
Bell would have fared in the major leagues if a team owner had
had the courage to violate baseball's unwritten whites-only rule
before 1947. *Photo by Pete Souza*

Lake Orion, Michigan

"I work here seven days a week," says the most famous doughnut shop owner in a small town between Detroit and Flint, as he plays catch with his grandson Michael. "At first, the transition from baseball was tremendously difficult; I was used to being around men, competitive men, all the time. I still wanted to get people out," says Mickey Lolich, who pitched in the major leagues for 16 years. Eleven years after retirement, Lolich reports that he's adjusted now to life outside the game. "I'm only 20 pounds over my playing weight," he adds proudly. "And it's not from doughnuts, because I eat maybe two a day. It's from lack of exercise." *Photo by Randy Olson*

"Baseball is the only game left for real people," said the late Bill Veeck. "To play basketball, you have to be 7'6". To play football, you have to be the same width." Clockwise from top left:

Durham, North Carolina *Photo by Andy Levin*

Detroit, Michigan *Photo by Pauline Lubens*

Oakland, California *Photo by John W. McDonough*

Lake Worth, Florida *Photo by Randy Olson*

Bradenton, Florida *Photo by Joe Traver*

Tampa, Florida *Photo by Bradley Clift*

A Giant Passion

From an interview with Tom Curley, President and Chief Operating Officer, USA Today

For 100 years there have been Giants fans in my family, beginning with my great-grandfather. They were all railroad people and they could go anywhere they wanted, free, so they went around to games. My grandfather took my mother to the World Series in Boston in 1915. She was three years old. Years later he taught me at the kitchen table, going over the box scores. He would be eating sauerkraut and beer and hotdogs for breakfast. He was a tough old guy. That was 1954, and

he was living and dying with the Giants, the year they won it all. If we were listening on the radio at home, I was the "luck element." They had a red chair and would call me in if the Giants got behind and I would sit in the red chair until the Giants got ahead. And the Giants turned around a lot of games that year. The *winning* is what captivated me.

When the Giants moved to San Francisco I gravitated with them. There was no way I would have rooted against Willie Mays. Ultimately, I think baseball often comes down to one individual player's grip on your psyche. I read every article on Willie Mays over the years, and I'm now reading every article on Will Clark.

Baseball is life. Every day you read the scores and they connect you to life, to people, to little cities, to big cities. Last year I decided to take my older daughter on an odyssey. I took her out of school and we went to the playoffs at Wrigley, then to the SkyDome in Toronto, then to the citadel of the game, Candlestick. By the third day she was jumping and cheering—totally corrupted.

St. Petersburg, Florida
Ninety-eight-year-old catcher George Bakewell (*right*) poses for a portrait before one of the 60 games held each year between the Kids and the Kubs in the country's oldest softball program for senior citizens. Only players who are at least 75 years old are considered for membership in one of the two St. Petersburg teams, which leave Florida in the hot summer months to take on challengers throughout the country. Above, the 34 members of the Kids & Kubs, average age 81, parade around the diamond in a ritual that precedes each game. *Photos by Rick Rickman*

Helena, Oklahoma

Most baseball fields have fences, but few are as imposing as those at the James Crabtree Correctional Center. Inmate teams from across Oklahoma converge several times a year for slow-pitch softball tournaments, usually traveling to the host institution shackled hand and foot. "It's a privilege to play in these tournaments," says Bobby Craft, the recreation director at the medium-security state reformatory in Granite, a three-hour drive from Helena. "It's the only thing the inmates look forward to. They'd do anything to go." Craft selects his team from the best players in the 10-team intramural league at the Granite reformatory, taking care to put together a team with a healthy racial balance—and with as few discipline problems as possible. "When I pick the all-star team," he says, "I look for guys with good attitudes"—such as Freddie Stimpson and Donnie Johnson, sharing a smoke, or Skip Jamison, smoking a pitch. But just in case, play is interrupted every half-hour to count and search the inmates. *Photos by Brian Payne*

Washington, D.C.

In a town where everyone plays hardball—and from which two different major league teams called the Senators moved away in the 1960s and 1970s because of low attendance—the highlight of the year comes each August, when Congressional Republicans square off against their Democratic colleagues at Four Mile Run Park in Alexandria, Virginia. Like Jack Buechner (R-Missouri), who does some last-minute scouting on his car phone (*above*), most participants in the annual Congressional Baseball Game wear the uniforms of teams that play in or near their districts. Says Cardinals fan Buechner: "We play to win, and we're more prone to taking risks than pro athletes because we do it for our egos, not our business. Nobody wants to embarrass himself." A catcher in previous years, Buechner now serves as designated hitter: "I tore a rotator cuff throwing candy in a parade," he says. "It's the ultimate political injury, sort of like breaking a finger shaking hands." Back on Capitol Hill (*right*), player-manager Martin Sabo (D-Minnesota)—a Twins fan who is no relation to Cincinnati Reds star Chris Sabo—hopes his charges can sock it to the GOP in a game that will determine the winner of the Roll Call trophy, given at the end of every five-year cycle. *Photos by Annie Griffiths Belt*

Fairbanks, Alaska
Above: Up past their bedtime, young scouts present the colors at midnight on June 21 during the feature game of the summer league in Alaska. College players come from around the country to play ball under the sun all day—and all night—long. *Photo by George Steinmetz*

Alexandria, Virginia
Right: As the members of Congress stand for "The Star Spangled Banner" before their annual game, late arrival Fred Upton (R-Michigan) emulates the fictitious Joe Hardy, lead character in the Broadway play and hit movie *Damn Yankees*, who was known as "Shoeless Joe from Hannibal, Mo." *Photo by Annie Griffiths Belt*

Joel Meyerowitz

The Joys of Summer

From an interview with Calvin Hill, former professional football player; Vice President for Personnel, Baltimore Orioles

Football is a lot like being on the corner of 57th Street and Fifth Avenue in Manhattan at twelve noon. There's a lot of energy and a lot of things happening. Baseball is sitting on the front porch, drinking lemonade, listening to your father talk to his father or his brothers about the game and things that happened that day. Part of the appeal of baseball now is that it's a reminder of the ways things used to be before we became so transient, so mobile, so much in a hurry. Baseball is stopping by the fence to visit; football is honking the horn.

Before batting practice, baseball players are kidding around, maybe talking to the fans, while in a football locker room it's like getting ready to jump out of an airplane, or going into battle. Everybody's in his own world, trying to blot out what's about to happen. Baseball players are intense at getting themselves ready, but by comparison with football players they're a bunch of guys getting ready to go fishing or hunting.

Eugene, Oregon
Left: Hungry fans step up to the plate at a July 4th picnic in the Beaver State's second-largest city, home to the Emeralds of the Class A Northwest League. *Photo by Robb Kendrick*

Orleans, Massachusetts
Previous page: The red-white-and-blue bunting on the outfield fences signals that this is a playoff game, as the Orleans Cardinals host the Yarmouth-Dennis Red Sox in the Cape Cod League. College players from across the country show their stuff to residents and major league scouts alike in the invitation-only summer league; during the 44-game season, the players from the 10 teams live with local families and work part-time in local stores and factories. About 10 percent of the players on major league rosters are veterans of the league, which dates back to the 19th century. *Photo by Joel Meyerowitz*

Westphalia, Iowa

The concept of the "farm team" takes on new meaning in the amateur Iowa Western League. Most of Westphalia's residents grow corn and beans, or raise hogs and cattle—and most of the younger men aspire to a place on the town team, the Red Sox. The Westphalia baseball field is the town's primary gathering place (*above*), with the scratchy scoreboard getting a workout from the games that tie up the field all day every day during the summer (*above, right*). For those who can't get away from their chores and get out to the ballpark, Red Sox games go out over the airwaves (*right*). *Photos by David Peterson*

Bismarck, North Dakota
On the run: dashing out of the stirrups at a softball tournament (*left*)... *Photo by John Biever*

New York, New York
... high-stepping with a laugh as Little League parents take their turn at bat (*above, right*) ... *Photo by Robert Maass*

Albuquerque, New Mexico
... and rounding first during a beep baseball contest (*right*). *Photo by Judy Griesedieck*

Bismarck, North Dakota
Top left and above: For thousands of players in the Midwest, the softball season reaches its climax with the annual Sam McQuade Charity Softball Tournament in June. More than 400 teams ranging from the Beulah Gasification Outlaws to the Dickinson German Hungarian Club take part in the marathon competition, which runs from 7:00 a.m. to 10:00 p.m. over two days on 28 diamonds. Once all the trophies have been handed out and the cheering is over, the big winners are local and regional charities: Over $25,000 is raised in a typical year. Although many more teams would gladly take part, the number of entrants is limited pending construction of more ballfields. *Photos by John Biever*

Atlanta, Georgia
The sweet spoils of victory: Arnold Heidt of the County Reds seeks out his wife Sharon after a softball game with the Atlanta Twins (*left*). *Photo by Judy Griesedieck*

Sponsor

Eastman Kodak Company

Major Contributors

The National Sports Daily
The New Lab
Pallas Photo Labs, Inc.

Contributors

Abaton
Adobe Systems
Aldus Corporation
American Sports Medicine Institute
Apple Computer, Inc.
Barneyscan Corporation
Baseball America
Boston Red Sox
CBS Sports
Chicago Cubs
Color 2000
Copy Service
Crent Company
Dixie League Youth Baseball
The Eddie Adams Workshop
Elizabethton Twins
Farallon Computing, Inc.
Harlem Little League
Hillerich & Bradsby Co., Inc.
Kids & Kubs
Kielty & Dayton
The Laser Toner Refill Company
Little League Baseball
Los Angeles Dodgers
The Maine Photographic Workshops
Major League Baseball
Major League Scouting Bureau
Major League Umpire Development
  Program
Mississippi State University
National Association of Professional
  Baseball Leagues
National Baseball Hall of Fame
Oakland Athletics
Oklahoma State Reformatory at Granite
Omnicomp
Pinnacle Publishing Services
PrintMasters
The RxMedia Group
Salt Lake Trappers
Smithsonian Institution National
  Associate Program
Society for American Baseball Research
Specialized Messenger Service
Sports Illustrated
Sportsworld
University of Georgia Sports Information
Waldeck's
Wetmore School
Yakult Swallows

Friends, Advisers and Consultants

Robert Adair
Chuck Adams
Paul Alexander
Carlos Alfonso
Rebekah Allen
John Altberg
Jay Alves
Dave Alworth
Rick Amos
Diana Anderson

William Arlt
Dave Aust
Gene Autry
Ralph Avila
Karen Bakke
Anna Maria Bambara
Howard Barney
John Baxter
John Bergez
Yogi Berra
Vince Bielski
John Billings
Peter Bjarkman
John Blake
Gene Blumberg
Billy Bock
Dick Bogard
Cecilia Bohan
Amy Bonetti
Katherine Boschetto
Roger Bossard
Edward & Esther Bourg
Dick Bresciani
Darryl Brock
Ray Broekel
Heather Brown
Russell Brown
Ben Buckley
Rich Busse
Alexander Cartwright
Bo Cavin
Orlando Cepeda
Dave Chambers
Ed Cheff
Victor Chiles
Albert Chu
Beth Churchill-Fantz
John Claffey
Richard Clelland
Prudence Clendenning
Bill Clouser
David Cohen
Carole Coleman
Ned Colletti
Dottie Collins
Cathy Corcoran
Bobby Craft
Mike Cramer
Cindy Crawford
Ron Cuffe
Tom Curley
Paula David
Ray DeMoulin
Bob DiBiasio
Joe Dier
Charles Dillman
Dennis Dimick
Sheila Donnelly
Gene & Gayle Driskell
Joel Drucker
Carmon Dugger
John Earhart
Gloria Eckert
Morris Eckhouse
Steve Edelman
Ron Enriquez
Ellen Erwitt
Elliott Erwitt
Jeanette Erwitt
Dan Evans
Dan Ewald
Jeanne Farrugia
Katy Feeney
Jim Ferguson
Matt Fischer
Kim Fitzharris
Susan Fornoff

Brian Foster
Jill Fox
Agnes Frakes
Laurel Frankel
Jeff Freeman
Ira Gabriel
Rebecca Gardner
Matt Gerszewski
Al Gonserowski
Steve Goodman
Stephen Jay Gould
Bill Granger
Rich Griffin
Bill Guilfoile
Tony Guzman
Jerry Hall
Tim Hamilton
Cara Haney
Timothy Hardy
Chris Harrington
Tom Harris
Steve Haugen
Chuck Heberling
Tom Heitz
Hugh Helm
Tina Helsell
Calvin Hill
Darren Hodges
Sam Hoffman
Leif Hope
Jay Horwitz
Neil Hoyt
Ron Hussey
Jeff Idelson
Ike Ikuhara
Ed Inouye
Sharlene Itoman
Phil Jache
Kathy Jacobson
Bill James
Charles Jennings
Duffy Jennings
Jim Jennings
Frank Jernigan
Joan Jett
Frank Jobe
Walt Jocketty
Tom Johnson
John Jonas
Elvis Jones
Ken Jones
Amy Kalonick
Troy Kashon
Chief Kawako
Steve Keener
Kate Kelly
Robert Kennedy
John Krich
Tom Kunhardt
Charles Kuralt
Jim Lachimia
Carlos Ladezma
Wendy Lagerstrom
Chuck LaMar
Stuart Lamb
Dan Lansing
Edwin Lawrence
Billie Jeanne Lebda
Bonnie Legg
Richard Levin
Jerry Lewis
Arsenio Lopez
Geraldine Lopez
Richard Lovrin
Mitch Lukevics
David Lyman
Ron Maestri

Chris Magdaleno
Marta Mansfield
John Maroon
Julius Mason
Lucienne & Richard Matthews
Rob Matwick
Luis Rodriguez Mayoral
Michelle McCord
Hal McCoy
Drew McEachern
Mark McGwire
Walt McKeel
Andy McKnight
Cindy McManus
Sam McQuade, Jr.
Sam McQuade, Sr.
Tom Mee
Phyllis Merhige
Wayne Metcalf
Gary Migdol
Amy Miller
Don Miller
Donna Miller
Eileen Miller
Sid Miller
Joel Millman
Naomi Honda Mix
Scott Mlyn
Phillip Moffitt
Mike Moore
Ann Moscicki
Raymond Mungo
Jeff Murphy
Mike Murphy
Dave Nahabedian
Mike Nayman
Matthew Naythons
Peggy Noonan
Kirt Ojala
Dan Okrent
Peter O'Malley
Brian O'Reilly
Dan Oshima
Salo Otero
Rusty Pallas
Daniel Paul
Lou Pavlovich, Jr.
Francisco Peña
Rich Pilling
Armand Plasencia
Christine Preble
Charley Pride
Klaus Priebe
Don Pries
Iris Raiford
Ray Razon
Gary Reed
Sarah Reiner
Richard Reynolds
Doug Rice
Thomas P. Rielly
Bill Rigney
Wes Rinker
Tim Roberts
Dave Robertson
Scott Rogers
Tom Romenesko
Rob Rose
Joan & Bob Rosenberg
Bari Rubin
Mark Rykoff
Pearl Sandow
John Schaffer
Kyle Scharhag
Alex Schober
Don Schomers
Ken Schreiber

Ron Schueler
Jim Schultz
Jim Schwendeman
John Sculley
Gerald Scully
Tom Seeberg
Mike Shannon
Ron Shelton
Larry Shenk
Brent Shyer
Allan Simpson
Larry Sindell
Harghajan Singh
Tom Skibosh
Marc Slaboni
Cork Smith
Karen Smith
Ray Smith
Tal Smith
Marvin & Gloria Smolan
Rick Smolan
Martin Snap
Michael Snowden
Paul Snyder
Eric Solomon
Matthew Sorrenti
Juan Sosa
Art Spander
Valerie Speiss
Pete Spence
Suzi Sperry
David Spitzler
Kim Springer
Randy Springer
Howard Starkman
Hollis Stein
Anne Stovell
Lew Stowbunenko
Andy Strasberg
Steve Streeter
Charles Styles
Belmor Sulit
Charles Sundling
Mike Swanson
Martin Swig
Michael Tchao
Studs Terkel
Melvin Thomas
John Thorn
Dick Thornburgh
Jules Tygiel
Della Van Heyst
Vea Van Kessel
Rick Vaughn
Fay Vincent
Dean Vogelaar
Greta Vollmer
Kara Waxman
Jeff Wehling
Walt Weiss
Steve Weller
David Wieland
Gwenne Wilcox
Hal Willard
Bill Williams
Mike Williams
Dave Willman
Don Winslow
Miles Wolff
Simon Worrin
Jim Wright
Kate Yuschenkoff
Paul Zingg
Richard Zitrin
Ben Zuniga

Photographers

Eric Lars Bakke
Nicole Bengiveno *New York Daily News*
P.F. Bentley *Time*
Susan Biddle *White House*
John Biever *Sports Illustrated*
Carrie Boretz
Michael Bryant *Philadelphia Inquirer*
David Burnett *Contact Press Images*
Joe Cavaretta *San Jose Mercury News*
Rich Clarkson
Bradley Clift
Jay Dickman
Elliott Erwitt *Magnum*
Misha Erwitt *Magnum*
Melissa Farlow *The Pittsburgh Press*
Natalie B. Fobes *Allstock*
Bill Frakes
John R. Fulton Jr.
Judy Griesedieck
Annie Griffiths Belt
Skeeter Hagler
Patrick Harbron *Outline*
Paul Harris
Ethan Hoffman
David Allen Hutson
Jeff Jacobsen *Topeka Capital-Journal*
Lynn Johnson *Black Star*
Karen Kasmauski
Ed Keating
Richard D. Kelly
Robb Kendrick
Mitch Kezar
Heinz Kluetmeier *Sports Illustrated*
Andy Levin
Caryn Levy
Tom Levy *San Francisco Chronicle*
V.J. Lovero
Pauline Lubens
Robert Maass
Rick Mariani
Richard Marshall *St. Paul Pioneer Press*
Chris Maynard
John W. McDonough *Sports Illustrated*
Joe McNally *Sygma*
Jim Mendenhall
Doug Menuez *Reportàge*
Joel Meyerowitz
Peter Read Miller *Sports Illustrated*
Ronald C. Modra *Sports Illustrated*
George Olson
Randy Olson *The Pittsburgh Press*
Brian Payne
David Peterson
Jim Richardson *West Light*
Rick Rickman
Steve Ringman
Monty Roessel
Lee Romero
Joe Rossi *St. Paul Pioneer Press*
John Shaer
Bill Smith
Chuck Solomon
Harley Soltes
Pete Souza
George Steinmetz
John Storey
Damian Strohmeyer *AllSport*
Patrick Tehan
Joe Traver *Gamma-Liaison*
Jerry Valente
Dan Warsinger
Hank Young *Young Company*
Michael Zagaris *Oakland Athletics*

Project Staff

Editorial Director
Karen Mullarkey

Project Director
Jennifer Erwitt

Managing Editor
Bill Messing

Design Director
Jennifer Barry

Director of Photography
George Olson

Writer
Bernard Ohanian

Interviewer
Mike Bryan

Assignment Editors
Gene Sunnen
Christopher Noble

Picture Editors
Barbara Baker Burrows, *Life*
Randy Miller, *Detroit Free Press*
Karen Mullarkey, *Sports Illustrated*
George Olson, *George Olson Photography*

Production Director
Lynne Noone

Design Assistants
Cecile Chronister
Kari Perin

Production Assistants
Diana Jean Parks
Stephanie Sherman
John Clay Stites

Film Traffic Coordinator
Andrew J. Hathaway

Researcher
Robert Ivry

Illustrator
Wendy Lagerstrom

Consulting Editor
Leonora Wiener

Copy Editor
Janice Maloney

Proofreader
Jonathan A. Schwartz

Collins Publishers

Publicity Director
Patti Richards

Sponsorship Director
Cathy Quealy

Sales Director
Carole Bidnick

Business Manager
Peter Smith

Sponsorship Manager
Blake Hallanan

Special Sales Manager
Jennifer Ward

Office Manager
Linda Lamb

Senior Accountant
Jenny Collins

Sponsorship Coordinator
Monica Baltz

Assistant Sales Manager
Maria Hjelm

Publicist
David Carriere

Administrative Assistants
James Kordis
Scott MacConnell
Jill Stauffer
Timothy Youmans, Jr.

Attorneys
Coblentz, Cahen, McCabe & Breyer, San Francisco

Sales Representatives
Mid-Atlantic
Robert Eickemeyer
John Leibfried
Frank Rizzo
Geoffrey Rizzo
Midwest
Leah Berg
Jim Lauber
Betty Redmond
Gene Rotenberg
Mountain States
Gordon Saull
New England
Joan Emery
Sam Prosser
Marc Seager
Northwest
Ted Lucia
Southeast
John Genovese
John Mackey
Edward Springer
Southwest
Michael Donahue
Bill McClung
Jim Shepherd
Edward Wood, Jr.
West Coast
Bob Ditter
William Maher
Thomas McFadden
Judy Wheeler

Amilcare Pizzi s.p.a.
Germano Barban
Bruno Bernini
Gilberto Costa
Sandro Diani
Giuseppe Gaiani
Elena Gaiardelli
Alberto Giacomazzi
Mary Lapegna
Fortunato Lessio
Sergio Marazzi
Gilberto Moro
Bruno Nicolis
Massimo Pizzi
Rodolfo Pizzi
Barbara Sadick

Editors' Note

This book is the product of a collaborative effort among literally hundreds of individuals all over the United States. As Assignment Editors Gene Sunnen and Chris Noble scoured the country to find the stories that define baseball in America, they met and spoke with countless people who freely offered their knowledge, their enthusiasm, their ideas, and their support. One day it might be the groundskeeper at a park in Florida, the next a Little League parent in Wyoming or a minor league bus driver in New York. Many became key contacts for project photographers as they traveled about the country; others provided indispensable information during the research process as the book was laid out. In time we came to see this network as a pattern for the book itself, bringing together people who might otherwise have nothing in common but who share a simple love for the game. We can't name them all here, but hope that each will see a little of himself or herself in the photographs that make up the book. To all, our deepest thanks.

This book was designed and produced entirely on Apple Macintosh II computers using Mass Microsystems external hard drives with removable 45-megabyte DataCart cartridges. The images were digitized with both a Barneyscan and an Abaton 300 scanner. Output was generated using Adobe type fonts on a Linotronic L-300 printer. Project software included Aldus PageMaker 4.0, Adobe Illustrator 88, Living Videotext's MORE, and Microsoft Works. Collins Publishers has a local area network utilizing Farallon Computing's PhoneNET PLUS and THINK Technology's InBox to link 30 Macintoshes. We gratefully acknowledge the companies listed here for their assistance.

Bill Frakes